ISRAEL
the land

Debbie Smith

A Bobbie Kalman Book

The Lands, Peoples, and Cultures Series

Crabtree Publishing Company
www.crabtreebooks.com

The Lands, Peoples, and Cultures Series

Created by Bobbie Kalman

Coordinating editor
Ellen Rodger
Proofreader: Adrianna Morganelli

Project development, writing, editing, and design
First Folio Resource Group, Inc.
Pauline Beggs
Tom Dart
Marlene Elliot
Kathryn Lane
Debbie Smith

Revisions and updates
Plan B Book Packagers
Redbud Editorial

Special thanks to
Shawky J. Fahel, J. G. Group of Companies; David H. Goldberg, Ph.D., Canada-Israel Committee; Steven Katari; Taali Lester, Israel Government Tourist Office; Alisa Siegel and Irit Waidergorn, Consulate General of Israel; and Khaleel Mohammed

Photographs
Steven Allan: p. 11 (top and middle), p. 12, p. 18 (top), p. 21 (top); Pavel Bernshtam/Shutterstock, Inc.: p. 17 (top right); Van Bucher/The National Adubon Society Collection/Photo Researchers: p. 25 (bottom right); Odelia Cohen/Shutterstock, Inc.: p. 31; Bruce Coleman Inc.: Eitan Simanor: cover; Mike Donenfeld/Shutterstock, Inc.: p. 26 (bottom); Joel Fishman/Photo Researchers: p. 21 (bottom right); Baruch Gian/Consulate General of Israel: p. 17 (bottom); Rostislav Glinsky/Shutterstock, Inc.: p. 11 (bottom), p. 13 (bottom), p. 16; Louis Goldman/Photo Researchers: p. 8 (top), p. 19 (bottom); Tibor Hirsch/Photo Researchers: p. 19 (top); Shootov Igor/Shutterstock, Inc.: p. 13 (top); Israel Government Tourist Office: p. 8 (bottom), Boris Katsman/Shutterstock, Inc.: p. 18 (bottom); kavram/Shutterstock, Inc.: p. 1; Nir Levy/Shutterstock, Inc.: p. 14 (bottom); Stella Levi/Shutterstock, Inc.: p. 22 (bottom); Mikhail Levit/Shutterstock, Inc.: p. 17 (left); David Mail/Shutterstock, Inc.: p. 26 (top); NEO/Shutterstock, Inc.: p. 10 (top and bottom); Richard T. Nowitz: p. 3, p. 7 (bottom), p. 9 (left), p. 14 (top), p. 15 (top), p. 20, p. 21 (bottom left), p. 22 (top), p. 23, p. 24, p. 31 (bottom); Richard T. Nowitz/Photo Researchers: p. 29; Mark D. Phillips/Photo Researchers: p. 9 (right); Nola Rin/Shutterstock, Inc.: p. 13 (middle), p. 15 (bottom), p. 28 (top); Jerry Shulman/Visual Contact: p. 22 (bottom); Inga Spence/Tom Stack & Associates: p. 7 (top); Steffen Foerster Photography/Shutterstock, Inc.: p. 20; Josef F. Stuefer/Shutterstock, Inc.: pp. 4-5; Rob Swanson/Shutterstock, Inc.: p. 10 (middle), p. 30 (right); Lopatinsky Vladislav/Shutterstock, Inc.: p. 29; Arkadiy Yarmolenko: p. 30 (top); Laura Zito The National Audubon Society Collection/Photo Researchers: p. 25 (top)

Map
Jim Chernishenko

Illustrations
William Kimber. The sabra, or prickly pear cactus, appears at the head of each section. An ibex, a wild goat native to Israel, is shown on the back cover.

Cover
The Bell caves of Beit Govrin National Park are a series of 80 large caves connected by passageways. Crosses and Arabic inscriptions on the cave walls indicate they were dug many hundreds of years ago.

Title page
The Negev Desert makes up almost 70 percent of Israel's land surface. Several towns and at least two cities, Beersheba, and Eilat, are located in the Negev.

Library and Archives Canada Cataloguing in Publication

Smith, Debbie, 1962 Nov. 17-
Israel : the land / Debbie Smith.

(Lands, peoples, and cultures series)
Includes index.
ISBN 978-0-7787-9311-3 (bound).--ISBN 978-0-7787-9679-4 (pbk.)

1. Israel--Description and travel--Juvenile literature.
2. Israel--History--Juvenile literature. I. Title. II. Series.

DS102.95.S647 2007 j956.94 C2007-906229-6

Library of Congress Cataloging-in-Publication Data

Smith, Debbie, 1962-
Israel. The land / Debbie Smith.
p. cm. -- (The lands, peoples, and cultures series)
"A Bobbie Kalman book."
Includes index.
ISBN-13: 978-0-7787-9311-3 (rlb)
ISBN-10: 0-7787-9311-7 (rlb)
ISBN-13: 978-0-7787-9679-4 (pb)
ISBN-10: 0-7787-9679-5 (pb)
1. Israel--Description and travel--Juvenile literature. I. Title. II. Series.

DS107.5.S639 2007
915.694--dc22 2007041474

Crabtree Publishing Company
www.crabtreebooks.com 1-800-387-7650

Published in Canada
Crabtree Publishing
616 Welland Ave.
St. Catharines, ON
L2M 5V6

Published in the United States
Crabtree Publishing
PMB16A
350 Fifth Ave., Suite 3308
New York, NY 10118

Published in the United Kingdom
Crabtree Publishing
White Cross Mills
High Town, Lancaster
LA1 4XS

Published in Australia
Crabtree Publishing
386 Mt. Alexander Rd.
Ascot Vale (Melbourne)
VIC 3032

Contents

4 Shalom Israel!

6 The lay of the land

10 How low can you go?

12 Weather forecast

14 A diverse people

16 Cities ancient and new

18 Jerusalem, the city of gold

20 Digging up the past

24 Flora and fauna

26 Israel at work

30 Transportation

32 Glossary and Index

 Shalom Israel!

As you stroll through a walled city in Israel or wind your way through a bustling marketplace, you will hear friends, neighbors, and relatives calling out to one another *"Shalom!" "Salam!"* These are the Hebrew and Arabic words for hello, goodbye, and peace.

In this country with little water and a lot of desert, people have wrestled with nature to build towns and cities, farms and factories. Israel is a modern country with an ancient history. The state of Israel was founded in 1948, but the land has been home to many groups of people over thousands of years. It is a center of worship for three major religions: Judaism, Islam, and Christianity. It is also a **homeland** and a dream come true for millions of people.

The lay of the land

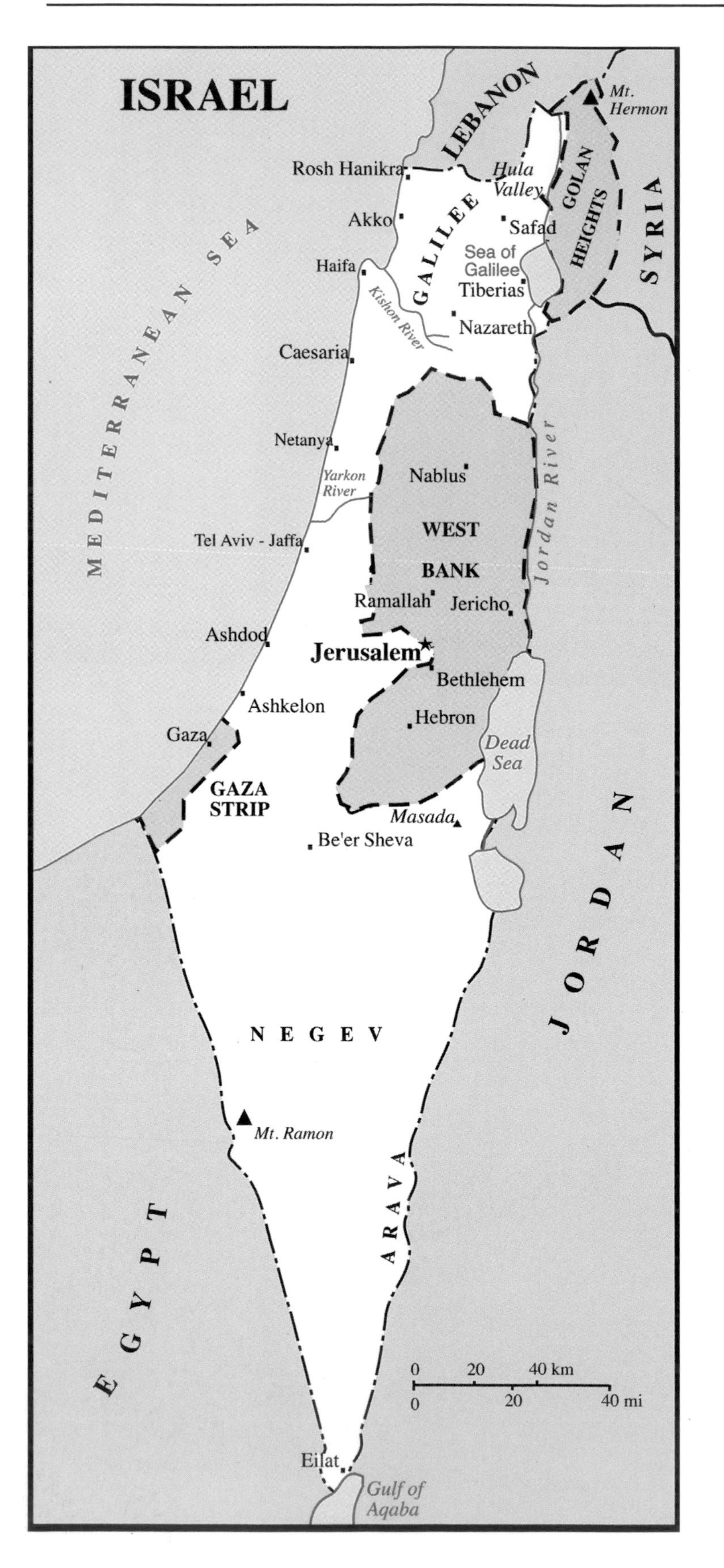

Israel is a sliver of land that is wedged between Jordan, Egypt, Lebanon, Syria, and the Mediterranean Sea. It is only 470 kilometers (290 miles) long and 135 kilometers (85 miles) wide. Its highest point, Mount Hermon, is a snowcapped mountain that rises to a dizzying height of 2,814 meters (9,219 feet). Its lowest point is the Dead Sea which plummets to an astonishing 400 meters (1,312 feet) below sea level. Israel's landscape is divided into four main geographical regions: the rift valley, the hills of Galilee, the coastal plains, and the Negev Desert.

A crack in the earth

Millions of years ago, the Earth's crust split and created a huge valley. This valley is known as the Great Rift Valley. It stretches from Syria in the north to Mozambique, in southern Africa, to the south. The Great Rift Valley follows a line along the entire eastern border of Israel. It passes through the Hula Valley, Sea of Galilee, Jordan Valley, Dead Sea, Arava Desert, and Gulf of Aqaba. Israel's main inland waters are located in the Great Rift Valley. The longest river is the Jordan River. As the Jordan River flows south, it feeds a lake known by three different names: the Sea of Galilee, Lake Tiberias, and Lake Kinneret. The Sea of Galilee is the lowest lake in the world and Israel's largest source of fresh water. Most of Israel is very dry.

(above) Israel's farms export everything from oranges to fish. These farms lie along the Jordan Valley.

(above) The Great Rift Valley passes through the Arava Desert in the south of Israel.

(above) The snowcapped peaks of Mount Hermon rise above Metulla, on the border with Lebanon.

The hills of Galilee

Steep cliffs, rolling hills, **fertile** valleys, and rivers cover the north and central parts of Israel. In the northwest, the limestone hills of Galilee drop into the sea. In the northeast stretch the Golan Heights, which were originally formed by ancient volcanic eruptions. Further south are rolling hills splashed with villages, olive groves, and **vineyards.**

(below) Two friends enjoy a stroll through the surf of the Mediterranean Sea.

The coastal plains

Many of Israel's first settlements were built on the coastal plains, which run along the Mediterranean Sea. Towns such as Jaffa and Akko became important port towns thousands of years ago. Today more than half of Israel's population lives in this region, with its white sandy beaches in the west and fertile farmland in the east.

The Negev

The Negev is a large desert that is shaped like an upside-down triangle. The northern and southern parts are very different. The north is covered with low hills and plains. Here the soil is powdery, yellow, and fertile. The south is filled with **plateaus** covered with rocks and deep canyons that cut the landscape. There are dry riverbeds called *wadis* and huge craters called *cirques*. From time to time, fertile spots called oases pop up. The oases are fed by underwater springs that help trees such as the date palm and fig tree grow and bear fruit.

(above) The waterfalls of Ein Gedi are a welcome relief from the scorching heat of the Judean Desert.

(above) Millions of years of** erosion **have sculpted King Solomon's Pillars from red sandstone cliffs.

How low can you go?

(above) Many people slather on the healing black mud of the Dead Sea.

(below) Road signs point to the lowest place on Earth.

The Dead Sea, in the Judean Desert, is not a sea at all. It is actually a huge lake with the saltiest water in the world. At 400 meters (1,312 feet) below sea level, it is also the lowest place on Earth.

The Dead Sea is fed mainly by the Jordan River. Once the water flows in, there is nowhere for it to go since water cannot flow upward and the Dead Sea is lower than the land around it. The trapped water **evaporates** in the heat and leaves salt and other minerals behind.

Swimming in salt

The Dead Sea is so salty that no fish or plants can survive in its waters. People swimming in the Dead Sea cannot sink. Instead, they bob around like corks. There are many Dead Sea health spas and hot springs. Some people believe that a float in the mineral-rich lake will make their aches and pains disappear. You have to be careful, though. The salt water stings and you may discover cuts that you never knew you had!

(below) The Dead Sea's salt content keeps swimmers buoyant, or afloat.

Harvesting the sea

The minerals from the Dead Sea are useful for more than healing bodies. Potash is used in **fertilizers** and **pesticides**. Bromine is used in the petroleum and chemical industries, in photography, and in medicine. Magnesium is used in fireworks and to build car and airplane parts. Increased use of water that flows into the Dead Sea has rapidly shrunk the sea. Israel and Jordan, which share a Dead Sea border, have discussed a plan to bring water from the Mediterranean or Red Sea to the Dead Sea through canals. The proposed Two Seas Canal plan would allow for new power and **desalination** plants. An agreement to study the plan was signed in 2005 between Israel, Jordan, and the Palestinian Authority. Environmentalists think the plan could forever alter the **ecosystem** of the area.

(top) The Dead Sea Works produces potash for over fifty countries around the world.

(right) Salt from the Dead Sea.

(below) The Dead Sea shrinks by three feet (one meter) a year because water flowing into it has been used for watering crops and other purposes.

 Weather Forecast 

Israel has two main seasons: a rainy winter season that lasts from November to April and a dry summer season that lasts from May to October. The **climate** varies from region to region, depending on how high up you are and how far you are from the sea. The coolest spots are in the hills and mountains to the north. The hottest spots are in low-lying areas, such as on the shores of the Sea of Galilee and in the Arava Desert. The north and west parts of the country get the most rain. The driest places are in the south and in the east.

Temperature highs and lows

	January		August	
	High	Low	High	Low
Safad	9°C (48°F)	4°C (31°F)	29°C (84°F)	18°C (64°F)
Eilat	21°C (70°F)	9°C (48°F)	39°C (104°F)	25°C (77°F)

Rainfall highs and lows

	Average number of days	Average amount of rainfall
Safad	75	718 mm (28 inches)
Eilat	8	25 mm (1 inch)

Children laugh and scream as they soak each other with a water hose on a hot summer day.

Flash floods

When a large amount of rain falls in a short amount of time, beware of flash floods! These floods rush down desert valleys and canyons. *Wadis* fill within minutes because the ground cannot absorb a lot of moisture. The floods are so powerful that they can uproot trees, shift boulders, and overturn cars.

Hold on to your hats!

A scorching wind blowing in from the Arabian Desert makes temperatures soar from May to June and again from September to October. This wind, called a *sharav* in Hebrew and a *chamsin* in Arabic, can last from two to five days. The *sharav* is so hot and dry that it destroys flowers and burns stalks of ripening wheat. Even the cows are affected by the heat. They produce almost fifteen percent less milk than usual unless they are in air-conditioned barns.

(top) Cool ocean breezes make coastal cities pleasant during the hot summer months.

(above and below) Israel's abundance of sunshine helps both its agriculture and tourism industries.

A diverse people

The people of Israel are as different and distinct as the country they live in. Some have lived on the land for generations. Others have **immigrated** to Israel from around the world.

Jews

Most Israelis are Jewish. Judaism is a religion whose teachings are based on ten commandments recorded in the Torah, the first five books of the holy Bible. The most important teaching is that there is only one God.

Jews first lived in Israel over 3,000 years ago. As different **empires** conquered the land, most Jews were **expelled** to other countries. Many faced great hardship and they prayed that they could one day return to their ancient homeland. The first wave, or Aliyah, of Jewish immigrants arrived in Israel from Europe in the 1880s. Other European Jews followed, as well as Jews from northern Africa and various countries in the Middle East. Jewish immigrants continue to arrive in Israel today, some still escaping hardship, and others wanting to live their dream by returning to their homeland.

(top) Almost 80,000 Ethiopian Jews came to Israel in the last two decades to escape war and *famine* ***in Africa.***

(right) This man keeps a store that sells prepared foods to people who have immigrated to Israel from all over the world.

Arabs

Arabs make up almost 20 percent of Israel's population. They ruled the country 1,500 years ago and have lived there ever since. Most Arabs are Muslims. They follow the religion of Islam and live according to the word of God, Allah, and the teachings of the **prophet** Muhammad. Muhammad received instructions from Allah on how to lead a good life. These instructions are written in the Qur'an, the Muslim holy book. Other Muslims are Christians. They follow the teachings of Jesus Christ, known to Christians as the Son of God. His life and lessons are recorded in the New Testament, the Christian holy book.

Before Israel became a country in 1948, the land was called Palestine. Today, many of Israel's Arabs still call themselves Palestinians.

(above) ***Sabra** is a nickname given to people born in Israel. They are said to be prickly on the outside and soft on the inside, just like the fruit of a sabra cactus that grows in Israel.*

(above) Bedouin women in traditional clothing.

Occupied Territories

When Israel declared its independence in 1948, the neighboring Arab countries declared war. Many Arab residents of Palestine left their homes during this war, called the War of Independence. Many of them settled in areas of Jordan, Egypt, Syria, and Lebanon that were close to the new country of Israel. Others remained in areas of Palestine that became part of Israel. After the Six Day War in 1967, Israel took possession of areas in the neighboring Arab countries where many Palestinians and other Arabs were living: the Sinai Desert, the Golan Heights, the Gaza Strip, the West Bank, and East Jerusalem. These are considered the "Occupied" or "Disputed" Territories. Since 1967, Israel returned the Sinai Desert to Egypt after a **peace treaty** was signed in 1979. In 1993, the Palestinians, who are still hoping to create their own state in the West Bank and the Gaza Strip, were given control of parts of these areas in a peace accord. The Palestinian Authority was created to help govern the area. Israel withdrew troops from the Gaza strip in 2005, but the final status of Palestine has yet to be determined.

Cities ancient and new

Some of Israel's cities are so old that you can see **synagogues**, **mosques**, streets, and city walls from hundreds, even thousands, of years ago. Other cities were once agricultural areas that grew as more and more people came to farm the land. To keep up with the need to house and create jobs for immigrants and **refugees**, Israel created development towns. Development towns were built mostly in rural or border areas.

Haifa, a port city

Haifa is located on the slopes of Mount Carmel and looks out over Haifa Bay. The center of Israel's technology industry, it is built on three levels. The port is on the lowest level. Shops, offices, restaurants, and older residential areas are on the next level up. The top level has many new neighborhoods, as well as some stores and restaurants.

Tel Aviv-Jaffa, the city that grew

The port town of Jaffa, on the Mediterranean Sea, is one of the oldest towns in the world. It is even mentioned in the Bible as the place from which Jonah set out, only to be swallowed by a whale.

In 1909, 60 Jewish families from Jaffa moved just outside of town. They founded the suburb of Tel Aviv. The suburb grew and grew until, in 1950, Tel Aviv-Jaffa became one city. Tel Aviv is the country's most important business center and is also the hub for shopping, theater, and sports. The busy Dizengoff Street is one of the best-known streets in Israel. In fact, in the Hebrew-language version of Monopoly, the name "Dizengoff" is used instead of "Boardwalk." Jaffa has many old buildings mixed with new ones, as well as galleries, cafés, and stores.

Israel's port cities are a contrast of busy commercial centers and old and new neighborhoods.

Be’er Sheva, the capital of the Negev

Be’er Sheva, in the northern part of the Negev, is built on a site that is over 3,500 years old. The city bustles with stores, museums, and university students. Its colorful Bedouin market competes for shoppers with newer shopping malls and plazas.

(above) You can buy anything from carpets to copper pots at an old market in Jerusalem.

(above) The ancient winding alleys of Jerusalem’s old city.

(right) Every Thursday morning hundreds of Bedouin gather at the desert city of Be’er Sheva’s market to sell clothes, spices, and livestock.

 Jerusalem, the city of gold

Jerusalem, Israel's capital city, is a mixture of cultures, religions, languages, and **traditions**. At over 3,000 years old, it is considered to be a **sacred** place by Jews, Muslims, and Christians. Jerusalem is divided into two parts: the old walled city and the new city outside the walls.

The Old City

The magnificent stone walls surrounding the Old City were built over 400 years ago. Eight gates lead into this part of Jerusalem, which is divided into four quarters: Jewish, Muslim, Christian, and Armenian. The old city's narrow, twisty roads are packed with small homes, markets, and shops. All the buildings are made of a rose-gold stone, called Jerusalem stone, that makes the city glow at night. Many of Jerusalem's most sacred sites are in the Old City.

(right) The Church of the Holy Sepulcher, rebuilt over ruins 800 years ago, holds the tomb of Jesus Christ.

(left) The Western Wall, also known as the Wailing Wall, is all that remains of the Second Temple. This Jewish holy site was destroyed by the Romans in 70 A.D. Every day Jews worship at the Western Wall. They slip prayers written on scraps of paper between the cracks of the wall in the hope that they will be answered.

The Dome of the Rock is sacred to Muslims. They believe that the prophet Muhammad rose from this site to heaven for one evening to meet with Allah.

Outside the walls

Outside the Old City is a vibrant modern city. The first neighborhoods were built outside the walls over 100 years ago. Today, the area includes office buildings, stores, restaurants, museums, and Israel's parliament, the Knesset. Several universities are located in Jerusalem. The Israel Museum and the Yad Vashem Holocaust memorial are also located in Jerusalem. Jerusalem is a center for soccer and basketball, Israel's favorite sports. Jerusalem is home to two major, and rival soccer teams.

(above) A major highway system runs just nine meters (30 feet) from the walls of the Old City.

Digging up the past

Archaeologists are explorers who seek out clues that tell how people lived, played, and worked in the distant past. They dig carefully through layers of earth and sand to find pots, weapons, works of art, and the remnants of buildings and towns. Israel has more than 3,500 archaeological sites where people have uncovered mysteries of past civilizations.

"Tel" all

Tels look like rounded hills popping out of flat plains, but when archaeologists start digging they find much more than just dirt. They discover towns that were built on top of each other over many centuries. Each town was abandoned, and sand and dust covered the houses and garbage left behind. Many years later, another town would be built in the same location. As archaeologists study a *tel's* layers, they learn how the culture of a people changed over time.

Archaeologists believe the caves at Mount Carmel, near Haifa, were used as dwellings 45,000 years ago.

Qumran

In 1947, a Bedouin shepherd boy was looking for his goat in a high hillside cave in Qumran, overlooking the Dead Sea. There he found some old jars with curious ancient scrolls. They were 2,000-year-old manuscripts. The manuscripts included the oldest surviving copies of the Bible and the writings of the people who lived in Qumran. Over the next nine years, archaeologists continued to dig. They found over 500 manuscripts in eleven caves. These manuscripts are known as the Dead Sea Scrolls.

Archaeologists **excavated** below the caves and found aqueducts, or channels for transporting water, and cisterns, which are tanks that hold water. They also discovered a kitchen, an assembly hall, council chambers, a pottery workshop, and the room where the scrolls were written.

(above) These archaeologists use picks to break through layers of rock. They are careful not to destroy an important finding.

(above) Piecing together fragments of the Dead Sea Scrolls is a time-consuming task.

(above) The caves where the Dead Sea Scrolls were discovered are near the tops of these hills.

(left) To reach the ruins of Masada, you can take a cable car to the top, hike up the winding Snake Path, or climb the much easier Roman Ramp.

Masada

Masada is the site of two ancient palaces built as part of a fortress by the Roman governor Herod the Great almost 2,000 years ago. The ruins are located on a mountain above the Dead Sea, 48 kilometers (30 miles) from Jerusalem. The fortress was taken over by Jews fleeing the Romans in 66 A.D. They lived there for six years before the Romans besieged the fortress and recaptured it. The Romans saw the Masada Jews as a threat to be controlled or eliminated.

The Romans set up eight camps around the base of Masada and built a ramp out of earth to the fortress walls. After eight months, they finally broke through the walls. Rather than surrendering, the Jews set fire to their homes and possessions and killed themselves. When the Romans captured the fortress the next morning, they found only two women and five children alive. The survivors had been hiding in a water pipe. Today you can visit the remains of Masada's palaces, swimming pools, lookout towers, and the oldest synagogue in the world.

(below) The stone walls of Masada are still remarkably strong after almost 2,000 years.

Caesaria

Herod the Great began building the city of Caesaria on the Mediterranean coast in 22 B.C. Archaeologists have uncovered remains of the many different civilizations who lived in this area before, during, and after Herod's time. The ruins of a hippodrome, a track for racing horses and chariots, lie between two modern roads. Roman aqueducts that once brought water to Caesaria from a nearby spring run along the ocean. A large moat and massive walls surround the remains of an ancient city, where the foundations of a Christian cathedral can still be seen. Outside the ancient city is a **Byzantine** street paved with marble slabs and protected by two headless marble statues.

Arched tunnels lead into the restored Roman** amphitheater **in Caesaria, where visitors today enjoy concerts, plays, ballets, and operas.

Flora and fauna

A large variety of plants and animals, or flora and fauna, make their home in Israel. Wildflowers of all kinds grow in the hills to the north where mountain gazelles roam. Bushy-tailed foxes and jungle cats travel the woods. Chameleons, gekkos, snakes, and other reptiles thrive in the desert where small shrubs and bushes grow.

Adapting to the desert

Plants in Israel have learned to **adapt** to the long dry spells in the Negev. Some seeds lie in the soil for years, waiting for a rainy winter before they all shoot up. Many trees and plants have deep roots so that they can search for water far underground. Small leaves on shrubs cut down on the amount of water that evaporates from the plant.

What happened to the trees?

Over 3,000 years ago, Israel was covered with oak, pine, and terebinth trees. By the early 1900s, most of these trees had disappeared. The armies of countries that **administered** the land of Israel had chopped them down to use as firewood and to prevent enemies from finding cover. Farmers had also cleared away trees to make room for farmland and grazing pastures for their animals. In the early 1900s, the Jewish National Fund (JNF) was founded to buy land for new farms and forests. Since then, the JNF has planted millions of pine and cypress trees. These trees help secure the soil so that wind does not blow it away. The trees also provide homes to small animals.

Some of the olive trees in the Garden of Gethsemane, in Jerusalem, are believed to be almost 2,000 years old.